From Brooklyn
to Liverpool

From Brooklyn to Liverpool

H. Ferebee Shephard

Library of Congress Control Number:		2019910617
ISBN:	Hardcover	978-1-7960-4868-1
	Softcover	978-1-7960-4867-4
	eBook	978-1-7960-4866-7

Print information available on the last page.

Rev. date: 07/25/2019

To order additional copies of this book, contact:
Xlibris
1-888-795-4274
www.Xlibris.com
Orders@Xlibris.com
799693

Chapter 1

Happy New Year! It was New Year's Day of 1943. Howard Carter Ferebee wasn't sure how he should participate in the war. Howard was a family man. He lived with his mother and sister on Herkimer Street in Brooklyn. He was a cook at one of the junior high schools in the community. On weekends, he cooked at the church when they needed him. He was also one of the first guys contacted when the young men in the neighborhood put together a game of ball. It didn't matter what kind of ball. Baseball, football, basketball—he loved to play them all. Then there were the ladies. Who was going to be the next Mrs. Ferebee was a question that wsas frequently asked by his mom and his lady friends. He felt there was no rush with so many candidates available.

Howard's life in Brooklyn was pretty good compared with anyone else in the working class of America, black or white. He had a good job, good family, good friends, and a dream for tomorrow. But the war interrupted many a young man's dream. Just like so many other young men in New York and around the USA, he thought he needed to do his part to defeat the Nazis. He thought about joining the army or marines or maybe the merchant marines. He knew the Nazis were evil and were filled with hatred.

The Nazis were trying to kill all the Jewish people in Europe and subject everyone who was not German to a subservient life. It was said that what they were doing to all of Europe was not that much unlike what he and his family and friends had to go through every day here in the USA. Or was it?

Howard was a young black man from Brooklyn, New York. He and others he knew suffered through job, housing, social, and economic segregation and discrimination for most of his life. Yet he felt that what he fought with here was a challenge that he and others could and would overcome with time and effort. As long as he was north of the Mason-Dixon line, it seemed that he and other Negroes were out of reach of the Ku Klux Klan and other hate groups here in the USA that thought black people had no right to exist.

There were small groups of Nazis here in the States, but they did little more than spout rhetoric. Black Americans had built this country on their backs and were entitled to everything the country had to offer. The problem was that not everyone had recognized that fact yet.

The Nazis had to be defeated. Howard knew he had to become involved, but he wasn't sure how. Living in Brooklyn, he knew a lot of young men who had joined the army and the merchant marines. He had to decide his route. The merchant marine was designed to assist commercial shipping and was not considered military, except during wartime. Well, this was certainly wartime.

Chapter 2

The duties of a merchant marine could be anything on a ship, and maybe even some military duties onboard, but that was not typical. He would talk with his mom and his sister because if he went to war, he would leave them alone. His dad had died of pneumonia some years before, and now he was the man of the house. His sister had recently graduated from college at New York University and would do well, he was sure. Their mom was in their house on Herkimer Street in Brooklyn and knew it was about time for him to step out and make a way for himself in the world and perhaps find a wife and start a family. Still, as a man and a citizen, he felt that he had to do his part. Maybe the merchant marines would be the best road for him. He wouldn't put himself in the line of fire, but he would work to supply the Allies with the tools they needed to fight the enemies. The opportunities for black young men were limited, even in the military, but growth was possible.

Howard wanted to continue his education and become an engineer. Perhaps he would be able to continue his growth in the merchant marines. Yes, that was the road he would take. For the next few nights, Howard lay in his bed and thought about what he thought his future would be. He would take a trip or two across the Atlantic Ocean, taking supplies to the Allies in Europe and doing his part to help defeat the Nazis. He didn't know what his role might be onboard a ship, but he was sure he would be able to put his mechanical skills to use.

He talked to his sister Ann to get her thoughts because he valued her opinion, and he thought she could be at least somewhat objective.

She mentioned some of the attributes of his plan but also some of the drawbacks. While it was true that it was a huge ocean and it might not be easy for the ship he would be on to be found and encountered by the enemy, if an encounter with an enemy plane or ship did happen, they would have to do their best to defend themselves, and they would undoubtedly be outgunned.

The Germans were known to patrol the North Atlantic in search of convoys to sink and destroy. The German U-boats had been fairly successful in their wolf-pack attacks. Still, these supplies for the allies had to get through. It was better for the Nazis to be defeated in Europe than they be allowed to flourish and perhaps invade the USA. Howard was sure the convoys would be protected because the supplies were so essential to the war effort. So at the end of January, he went to sign up for the merchant marines.

The sign-up was at the post office four blocks from his family's house. The process was brief, and they seemed anxious to get qualified young men both black and white. They asked how old he was and what he did for a living. Howard was almost twenty-seven and was currently working as a cook in a community school, but he was going to mechanics school at night. They didn't need any apprentice mechanics just now, but they did have a spot for a cook on a ship that was scheduled to sail in March. As soon as a mechanic apprentice spot opened up, he could apply for the opening, and he would be more likely to get it if already in the service. This made sense to Howard, so he enlisted as a cook.

Chapter 3

The ship Howard was assigned to was the USS *Harry Luckenbach*. It was to depart the Brooklyn navy yard on March 16, 1943. Howard, his sister Ann, and his mother had dinner together the night before. Together, they prayed for one another and asked God to protect them while they were separated.

The next morning, Howard reported to the shipyard to board the USS *Harry Luckenbach*. The ship left port and headed for the European continent. There were eighty men on board the USS *Harry Luckenbach*, and Howard and two other cooks prepared three meals a day for them. They had food that allowed them to fix pretty good meals. Howard enjoyed fixing dinner the most, but it seemed that the crew enjoyed all the meals equally. There was rarely anything left over. There were some crew members who seemed to show up looking for seconds after each meal.

The morning of the seventeenth started normally, with Howard and the other cooks getting up early to begin cooking breakfast. Howard liked the other cooks. One of them had been in the merchant marines for over two years. He had made three trips across the Atlantic and had been a cook back home in Maryland. He considered himself successful and was happy to be where he was. The other one had been a cook for six months, but this was his first transatlantic trip as it was Howard's.

The crew ate heartily, and the breakfast dishes were cleaned up. As had become his habit, Howard went up on deck to have a cigarette. As he was climbing the stairs, the ship's alarm sounded. They were under attack. It was a German U-boat. A submarine had been sighted. Two torpedoes were racing toward the ship. It was hard to see them because the sea was so rough. Seconds later, they struck the ship midway along the starboard side. The men on deck were scrambling for the lifeboats, but those who were below deck never had a chance.

Chapter 4

The ship was sinking fast. Howard was lucky because he had come up on deck for a smoke. Normally, he would have been down in the galley and would not have stood a chance of escaping. Howard and nine other crew members were working to get the lifeboat over the side and away from the sinking ship. As the ship was sinking, it created a vortex that almost sucked the lifeboat down too. There were other ships in the convoy, and they saw Howard's lifeboat and the one other lifeboat that made it off of the *Luckenbach*'s deck.

The torpedoes had hit the ship midway on the starboard side just below the water line, and it sank in only three minutes, so the men in the lifeboats were the only survivors. No other seamen were able to clear the ship's deck. With all of the chaos going on, it would be difficult for any of the other ships to pick up any survivors, if there had been any. There was one other lifeboat that made it over the side, but it only had six passengers. It was being tossed around on the rough water, and it didn't look like it would make it very far.

Howard's boat had several committed seamen who were determined that they would survive. The U-boat circled to attack other boats in the convoy. The other boats fired off depth charges trying to hit and sink the sub. The men in the lifeboat just paddled, trying to stay afloat and out of harm's way while the attack continued. It seemed like hours, but of course, it was not as long as it seemed. Finally, it was over. The men had managed to stay afloat and keep away from other torpedoes and depth charges, and now all they had to do was get to land and avoid any other German attacks.

The convoy had been heading east toward England and the European continent, but they had not been underway long enough for that to be an option for the little lifeboat. The men decided that their best option was to head north toward Iceland or Greenland. It shouldn't take more than a day or two to get there. The challenge would be to fight the rough water and stay afloat and stay warm enough to survive the trip to land. So they were underway. They would take turns with the oars, and Mike, the cargo loader, would be first.

Sal (short for Salvator) broke down. "Will we ever see our families again? What is going to happen to us?"

Howard spoke up. "We are alive. Whatever happens from here on will be God's will. He has seen us fit to put us on top of these waves and not under them, so let's be grateful and see what God has planned for us."

There were five guys who had been cargo handlers, three ship crew members, one security officer, and Howard. The lifeboat had some K-rations and some fresh water. Used sparingly, it should last them for a day or two. No one was thinking about food yet, but they were taking stock of what was there. They would have to make the best of what was there because there wasn't any fishing equipment on the boat.

Sal seemed to be the most nervous of the crew. Chris seemed to be the most nautically astute and tried to keep the boat headed in the right direction to go north. As they traveled, they saw some whales and some ships in the distance. They all thought about what they were leaving behind and what lay ahead. It was fair to say they were all nervous but to different degrees. Howard was putting his faith in God. Leland, one of the security guys, was intent on continuing the war, while Sal just wanted to go back home to New York. Conversation continued among the men about what they would do when they got back home, but no one doubted that they would get home. Some said they would rejoin the merchant marines, some said they would get out and join the army so they could fight back against the Germans, and some said they would just get out because they felt they had served their duty and time.

Howard wasn't sure. He thought about it and considered that he had only served briefly, but there were other things he wanted to do rather than continue to be a cook. The men continued to row and pray for help and the sight of land.

Chapter 5

***

Back in the States, every day, families were getting visits and letters from Uncle Sam about their loved ones who were killed or missing in action. It had only been a day or so, but the wheels of notification turned quickly when so many had seen the ship go down.

Two merchant marine officers were dispersed to the home of Ann Ferebee and her mother. There was a knock at the door. Neither Ann nor her mother had seen the government car pull up outside. "I'll get the door," said Ann. Expecting a neighbor or a friend, Ann opened the door with an expectant smile for the unknown visitor. Her smile quickly changed when she saw who it was.

"Ms. Ferebee, may we come in?" The two officers were very well dressed and professional-looking in their uniforms but stopped short of what one would call pleasant.

"Come in," Ann said. She turned her face from them and started to cry and called her mother into the living room.

From the kitchen, her mother responded, "Who is it, baby?"

Most of their friends would have come straight to the kitchen where something was usually on the stove. Her mother came into the living room to see who it was as the visitor wasn't going to the kitchen.

"Ladies, it is our very unpleasant duty to inform you that the USS *Luckenbach* has been sunk with all hands on deck. Your government offers you its condolences and appreciation for the service of your son and brother Howard Carter Ferebee. We respectfully ask that as you share the information of your loved one's demise, you limit the information that you share to avoid providing information that might benefit our enemies, such as the name of his ship or where it was and when it went down. He will be provided with a military funeral at no cost to you, his family, and his military life insurance will be made available to his beneficiary right away. Are there any questions we can answer for you?" the officer explained.

Ann and her mother just stood there, dumbfounded. They always knew that his death was a possibility but never really expected it to be a reality. Ann responded, "No."

The two officers stood and turned to leave. Her mother opened the door for them and walked quickly back to the kitchen. Ann closed the door behind them and walked through the living room where the bad news had just been shared to join her mother in the kitchen.

Chapter 6

***

Back in the small lifeboat, the men were rowing and looking north toward the coastline they hoped would be their next warm and peaceful port. The wind was cold, and so was the water. The men didn't talk much. Each was alone with his thoughts. Howard thought about his sister. *Would she stay in New York? Would she marry? What about Mom? Would she be OK? If Ann left New York, would Mom go too?* He was thinking about life in New York if he didn't get back. He wouldn't talk out loud about not getting back home, but he couldn't help but think about it. It was a possibility.

On the horizon to the north, the men could see a shoreline. It was a long way off, but they could see it. Also, in the distance, they could see a small sailboat, not very big but bigger than their small rowboat. They didn't think it was an enemy boat, but they didn't know who it was.

They kept rowing toward the shoreline. It seemed that the sailboat was on a course that would intersect with them. They continued to row and pray. It was almost dusk, and they didn't want to meet anyone who was not friendly until after dark. Being the smaller vessel, they felt if they needed to escape, their chances were better at night. The boat came nearer, and the men couldn't see any flags or sign that would identify the crew. As the boat drew nearer still, Howard and his crewmates began to yell greetings, hoping for a response that they could use to identify the oncomers as friends or foe. They could see men on deck but could not make out any responses.

Closer. Several men gathered on the other boat decks.

Sal yelled out, "Americans!"

Chapter 7

The men hesitated and then responded with what sounded like a friendly greeting, but it wasn't English. The men were waving and smiling, so Howard's boatmates relaxed a little. This could be a rouge to catch them off guard, but there didn't seem to be any weapons on the deck. As they drew alongside, the men continued to greet one another with friendly waves and smiles. They invited Howard and the guys to join them on board the sailboat.

"What do you guys think?"

"Well, I think we could take them if we had to as long as we stay together. I am ready to stand up. Let's do it."

The tired but confident men climbed onto the sailboat. The sailboat's crew welcomed the men on the boat, and they offered blankets and food, which the men readily accepted.

The food was different. It was bread and salted fish, with some fruits that were different from what they were used to. The boat resumed moving in the direction the rowboat had been traveling. The sailboat's crew was friendly enough, but none of them spoke English. They were white, but they didn't seem to act any differently toward Howard, which he appreciated.

The boat moved north toward the land that the men could see in the distance. The Americans were offered bread and salted fish and hot chocolate. It had been a number of hours since they had eaten anything, so they readily accepted and enjoyed it all. The men from the sailboat seemed relaxed and friendly enough; they exchanged pleasant smiles and laughter as the boat continued on its way. As they came closer to the land that the Americans anticipated to be their destination, they wondered what awaited them. They didn't know whether they were headed to Greenland or Iceland—both countries had been identified as friends of the Allies rather than the Axis, even though neither country was known to be particularly active in the war.

They could see the lights of a small fishing village. The men from the village began getting the boat ready to land. The men who were in charge made themselves obvious by instructing the crew as they all took to their tasks. The Americans just stayed out of the way as the others seemed very capable and worked very quickly as well.

The boat was steered into a small inlet and headed to a dock on the starboard side of the boat. Several men were on the dock, waiting to catch the ropes and tie the boat to the dock. The man on the boat who was in charge yelled to the men on the dock, and one of them turned and went up to the little building not far off the dock. Some of the seamen began unloading the ship's catch, and the others prepared the boat to be docked for the night. When they finished, they ushered the Americans off the boat.

By this time, quite a group had gathered to receive the newcomers. A rather tall man stepped to the front of the group and, in pretty good English, asked the Americans who they were and where they were from.

Sal, with his strong Brooklyn accent, spoke first. "We are Americans from the merchant marine ship USS *Luckenbach*. Our ship was torpedoed yesterday morning, and we are the only survivors as far as we know."

Chapter 8

The tall man spoke again. "You are here in the city of Sisimiut in the island nation of Greenland, and you are welcome. We are part of the nation of Denmark, and we do not look favorably on the Nazis and all that they are trying to do. We have radios here in town, so if you wish, we can contact your country and let them know you are here."

The men thanked the gentleman and relaxed for the first time in quite a while. Each of the men went away with some of the townspeople for the evening. Howard went with a fisherman named Thor. He lived a little ways off into town with his parents. When they arrived at his home, his parents warmly welcomed both Thor and Howard. They asked if they had eaten and had enough, and they had. The house was small but comfortable. They showed Howard to where he would sleep and made sure he was comfortable, and everyone turned in for the night.

In the morning, the household rose early. Thor's mom prepared breakfast for them all. After breakfast, Thor took Howard into town where he could look around and meet some of Thor's friends. Most of them were fishermen just like Thor and his father before him. There wasn't much need for machinists or mechanics in Thor's village.

Around midday, they went by the radio operator's shack to see what messages they had been able to send or receive. They learned that an English freighter headed back to England was due to come relatively close to Greenland the next morning. Howard began to think about it. He had been headed to England when they had been torpedoed anyway.

In England, he would certainly be able to catch a ride back home, either with a troop transport or a cargo vessel. He thought catching that ship would make much better use of his time than waiting for transportation headed in the other direction.

At the end of the day, everyone said their goodbyes and thanked their hosts and prepared to go out the next morning to meet the eastbound freighter. The next morning, all seamen were up with the sun and down to the dock as the fishing boat prepared to go out and meet the freighter. The fishing boat left the dock and headed south. They traveled for about forty-five minutes and then dropped their fishing nets. It got a little warmer as the sun rose on the eastern horizon, and they waited for a sign of the ship. To the north, they saw a pod of whales stirring up some fish for their breakfast. What they didn't eat would hopefully escape into the fishermen's nets. The fishermen went about their work as usual. The Americans watched and tried to stay out of their way. It was getting close to lunchtime and the time they expected the freighter. Shortly, they looked toward the western horizon and noticed a smoke plum.

Chapter 9

The fishing boat radio operator signaled the freighter, and they both corrected their path to intersect about a mile from where they currently sat. The two boats pulled alongside each other, and the freighter dropped a net ladder for the men to climb aboard. The Americans thanked their hosts for their hospitality and boarded the freighter. The freighter rode low in the water because it was loaded so heavily with war materials.

The men hoped they would not encounter any submarines for the remainder of their trip. The route they were taking was further north than the route they had taken with the *Luckenbach*, so they hoped the German submarines were patrolling the ocean further south. Normally, ships crossed the Atlantic as part of a convoy. They believed there was safety in numbers. This ship had left New York with only one companion ship because the cargo was very sorely needed and the next convoy wasn't due to leave for two weeks. The hope was that two ships traveling alone on the northern route would not attract any enemy attention.

Everyone kept their fingers crossed. The ship resumed its voyage with all the crew watching for other ships in any direction along the horizon. The ship continued to steam into the night. They anticipated that they would see England near the end of the next day. Time passed slowly, and the new passengers had no duties on board. Howard went below deck to see what they were carrying to England. There were several pallets of medical supplies, as well as vehicles and truck parts. A couple of other guys had come down as well. One of them spoke to

Howard and asked if he was looking for the kitchen. Howard told him no and that he had been a mechanic back in the States, and he wanted to look at the equipment the ship was carrying. His shipmate said they needed cooks much more than mechanics right now, so cross-training was not likely anytime soon. Plus, there had not been very many black mechanics in the merchant marines or civilian service from what he had heard. Those jobs were all going to the white boys. Howard ignored him and went back onto the deck above.

The men were shown to the quarters where they could bed down for the night, but most of them were not too excited about bedding down below deck given their very recent experiences. Howard stayed on deck with a couple of other boatmates. They talked into the night wondering what England was like and what the future held for them. They wondered how long it would be before they could hitch a ride back to the USA. The Nazis had already overrun Poland, and people wondered about North Africa. Eventually, the conversation turned back to home and missed loved ones. Howard thought about his younger sister. He knew that it was her desire to finish her education at New York University, and a life insurance payment would be a big help to her. He loved his little sister, but he wanted the best for her. She was focused on her education completely for the time being, and he wanted to help her as much as he could.

The morning was near now, and to the east, the men on deck could see the glimpse of the approaching sunrise and the western edge of the British Isles. They had made it safely, and now the next chapter of their lives was about to begin. The ship navigated its way into the harbor and to its docking port. All men helped with the unloading of the cargo, and then the men who had made this trip before led the way to the portside pub where the sailors grabbed a bite to eat and their first glass of ale since they last set foot on dry land. Howard went with the men but did not know what to expect. After all, in the States, the white and black sailors would drink at separate bars. They walked into the bar together, and the sailor named Jonathan with whom Howard had played chess called out, "Howard, come over here to my table."

Howard made his way through the crowd and joined his new friend. "You looked lost, so I thought you need a friend to share a stout one with," Jonathan said.

Howard said, "I just didn't know where the—"

"Stop right there. Things are a little different over here. The only sailors that can't drink one in any pub over here are the Germans. What will you have? The beer is on me tonight. I know you guys haven't tried your drink of choice."

They waved the barmaid over and placed their order. "Why don't you try some shepherd's pie too? It is one of my favorite dishes."

The men ate and drank and talked like two old friends for the next few hours. The captain had radioed ahead to the American counselor to arrange quarters for the *Luckenbach* shipmates, and the quarters were a couple of miles from the harbor. Howard's new friend knew that the quarters available for Howard would leave something to be desired, so he offered Howard space at his house under the guise of it being a much shorter walk from the pub. Howard gratefully accepted. The Englishmen both on the ship and at the pub treated Howard like how a shipmate or a neighbor would expect to be treated without regard to race or color.

When they arrived at his house, Howard noticed that it was not that different from his house in Brooklyn that he had shared with his mother and sister. "You can bunk in the first door at the top of the stairs to the left. My room is at the end of the hallway." Howard liked everything he had seen to this point in England. He asked if finding work would be difficult. Jonathan told him finding a civilian job should not be tough at all. Most of the English able-bodied men were in the military, so there was actually a shortage in the work force. The men turned in for the night and agreed to talk more in the morning.

Chapter 10

The next morning, Howard was the first one up and stepped outside on the front stoop. The neighborhood had already started to buzz. He noticed that Jonathan had a few nice-looking ladies for neighbors.

Jonathan soon came out and saw Howard noticing his neighbors. "None of them are married," he said. "They all work at the munitions factory. I will introduce you later if you like."

"Sure, that sounds fine," Howard said, and then he shrugged it off nonchalantly to show the relative unimportance of it.

Jonathan suggested for their morning meal that they go to a little breakfast tavern at the end of the row. They did, and the food was good. Jonathan didn't have to report to the dock for a few days because he had just come back from a trip. For the next few days, they just moved around town a bit and talked about the possibilities for Howard. He could go to the American consulate and resume his life in the States, or he could start a new life in England. The way he had been treated since his arrival in England led him to think that staying here would not be such a bad thing. The main thing that he needed to consider would be finding a job.

Jonathan had talked about a plant where they were working on everything from farm equipment to munitions and their need for mechanics and people with engineering inclinations. Howard asked Jonathan to show him where it was so that he could go and apply for work. He had just about decided to stay in England, but he had to find work before he could finalize that decision. Howard asked Jonathan for the loan of suitable clothes for a job-hunting expedition. Fortunately, they were close to the same size. Jonathan's pants were a little high water on Howard, but they would do. Howard went to the facility that he had been told had the most mechanical work opportunities. It was a big facility with several buildings and quite a few workers about. He went to the building with the administrative offices.

The personnel manager was in the first office with several subordinates. Howard spoke to one of the ladies and indicated that he was looking for work. "What can you do?" she asked.

Howard indicated that he had worked for about a year on a piece of machinery known to him as the big boy bender but actually named the Greenspan 335. It was a die-cut machine that they had used in Brooklyn. Howard noticed one in the building just outside of the admin building as he came in.

The lady called out, "Bill, here is one you can use." She was calling out to another placement officer in the office.

A man on the opposite side of the room looked up and waved for Howard to come over to his desk. "So you know the Greenspan 335?"

Howard answered in the affirmative.

"From where?" the man asked.

"I worked on it in Brooklyn, New York," Howard answered.

"It is not the newest machine out, but it serves our purpose. Any other machines?" the man asked.

"I have worked on a few, but I saw that one next door, so I thought I could help you with it."

"We had a guy who was really good with it, but now Her Majesty has him up near Liverpool. Where are you from?"

Howard thought for a minute then answered, "I came over on a convoy from USA. Word is you guys could use some help over here."

"Well, we can all use some help against these Germans. As long as we work together, we will beat them. Can you start this week?"

Howard answered, "I can start tomorrow if you like."

"Be here at 9:00 a.m., and report to Arthur in the mechanical section."

Howard thanked the personnel manager and left. He couldn't wait to tell Jonathan about his good fortune. The two men decided to go out for a celebratory dinner that evening, but they had to cut it short because the morning would come quickly.

The next morning, Howard was up at six o'clock. His new life was about to start. He stopped at the tavern at the end of the street to have some breakfast and then headed up the street to his new job.

When he got to the facility, he asked for Arthur. Arthur was a short man with a limp he got from fighting the Germans in France. He was a pleasant man with a ready smile. "May I assume you are the new man, Howard?"

"That's me," replied Howard.

"I understand you are familiar with the Greenspan 335."

"In New York, we called it the big boy bender."

"We call it that here too in the shop. I want to show you a couple of other machines as well. We stay quite busy here, making triggers for the new munitions system for the RAF. We'll show you the process, and you can get started on the swing shift. Mikal can get you started on the training for the different processes. Come on and meet the team first."

Howard met the members of the day shift and then went into the production wing with Mikal. There was a lot for him to see, but for the first week, Howard was asked to learn several processes and the operations of three different machines. Howard was thrilled at the opportunity and began to think he had made the right decision and England was going to work out.

Jonathan was scheduled for another trip the following week, so the guys went out again the last few days of the week. They went to another spot for dinner. The food was good, it was a Jamaican restaurant, but even better, there was a young lady there who seemed to watch Howard's every move. About halfway through dinner, she came over to their table and asked if he was from Jamaica.

"No, I am from Brooklyn, New York," he replied.

Chapter 11

She said she had a few cousins there but had never been there herself. Howard asked how long she had been in England and if she liked it. She said she had been here since she was thirteen, and it was pretty nice. There weren't very many young men here who got her interested, which is why she had summoned the nerve to come over to his table. Howard told her that she was glad she had. Her name was Claudia. Howard asked if they could set a date to meet for dinner later in the week and maybe spend some time together. Claudia said she would like that, and she left the men's table to rejoin her friends.

All the way back to Jonathan's house, they talked about Claudia and where he should take her the next time they were together.

The next morning, Howard went back to work. Today he was teamed with an older man named Stephan. They worked on a different machine. It seemed that management wanted to make use of Howard's overall mechanical ability, not just his familiarity with one specific machine. This was fine with Howard because he also felt the more he knew, the more valuable he was to the company. For the next few days, Howard worked on every machine in the facility and became comfortable with the company procedures.

As the end of the week approached, he was looking forward to seeing Claudia again. Finally, the day was here, and he hurried after work to meet her at the Jamaican restaurant. As he approached the restaurant, he spotted her waiting for him out in front. "Hi, Howard. Would you like English food or Jamaican food tonight?"

"Whatever you want is fine with me. I just look forward to being with you."

"Well, in that case, let's just walk and stop when we see something that looks interesting, OK?"

They strolled along the waterfront and into the Jamaican community. "Let's stop here. They have really good food. You will have to learn the difference between good Jamaican food and the rest," Claudia said.

They went into the restaurant and sat close to the front window. Claudia said she would order for both since he wasn't familiar with the menu. They started out with a rum drink while they waited for their food. "Jamaican rum is the best," Claudia said.

"That is the only kind my dad drinks. You will learn to love it as well."

Across the restaurant, Howard noticed a coworker at another table. He and his companion looked a little out of place as theirs was the only table occupied totally by nonblack customers. Some of the tables had mixed patrons, some were only black, but his coworker's table was the only totally nonblack table in the place. *Oh well, no big deal.* Howard thought. *Good food is good food.*

Claudia asked Howard what he thought of the food. He had thoroughly enjoyed the whole meal, and he said so. "Well, next time, I will take you to the best place in England. Not many people get a chance to eat there, so consider yourself lucky and special."

"I can't wait," replied Howard.

Claudia said it was getting late, and it was about time for them to wrap up the evening. She said she would walk Howard halfway back since the area was unfamiliar to him. They made plans for a trip to a museum the next day to look at some art.

The next day, they met around lunchtime and went to the museum. They had a nice afternoon, and then Claudia asked him if he was ready to try the best eating establishment in England, and of course, he was. Claudia took him through what she had told him was the Jamaican end of town. They went until they came to a small house toward the end of a narrow street. She opened the door and invited him in.

"My brother and I live here," she said. "He is on a weekend trip with his girlfriend. Make yourself comfortable, and I will get started in the kitchen."

The house was neat and clean but small. There was a lot around the room to remind one of Jamaica or at least what Howard imagined it to be like. The food was ready in short order.

"Dinner is served," said Claudia. It was an island meal with plantain and goat meat and a glass of rum to wash everything down. "In our family, the men have a smoke after dinner. Here is some of my brother's special tobacco. You will like it."

Howard put some in a pipe and lit it. After only one or two puffs, his head started spinning.

"How do you like it?" Claudia asked.

"This isn't regular pipe tobacco, is it?" Howard asked, even though he already knew the answer. Some of his friends in Brooklyn had told him about the marijuana, but he had never tried it before.

"It is regular in my country. My brother said it makes him hungry and makes him want a woman. You have already eaten, so I don't imagine it makes you hungry. Is what he says about it true?"

Howard said, "Come and sit by me and let's see."

The two spent the rest of the night wrapped in each other's arms.

The next morning, Claudia said, "If anyone asks me, shall I tell them that I am your woman, or was this just a fling for you?"

"I am your man if you want me," Howard replied.

"Good. Then we are one," Claudia responded.

Chapter 12

Howard went back to his house and told Claudia he would see her again in the evening. He stopped by the grocery store to pick up some food for the house. While he was in the store, he saw the same coworker again that he had seen in the restaurant while he was with Claudia the night before. This time he was by himself, but Howard had not noticed him in the neighborhood before.

The rest of the weekend went by without much ado. The next morning, Howard went to work, and his manager, knowing that he was new to the area, asked him how his weekend was. Howard responded that it was very nice and that he had seen one of his coworkers at a restaurant. His boss asked him who it had been, and Howard pointed him out.

"Are you sure it was him?"

"Yeah, I am sure. Why do you ask?" said Howard.

"I am just surprised as badly as he talks about the Jamaican people," replied his boss.

"I am sure it was him, and he was with another man I have not seen before."

This conversation stirred up Howard's curiosity, so he decided he would pay attention going forward. His coworker's hostility seemed out of place compared with the hospitality he had enjoyed otherwise since arriving in England.

At lunchtime, Howard thought he would see where the coworker went just out of curiosity. He followed him for a couple of blocks. He went into a building that didn't have a lunch facility in it, so Howard just watched from across the street. After a few minutes, he emerged from the building with the same man he had eaten dinner with the few nights before. They walked slowly in the direction of the plant and then parted company about a block before getting back to the facility.

Howard kept walking as his stomach reminded him that he hadn't had lunch yet. That evening Jonathan was due back from his trip, and the two friends were scheduled to eat together. Howard decided he would introduce his friend to the Jamaican restaurant he had enjoyed with Claudia. He was looking forward to telling his friend about his relationship with Claudia.

At the end of the day, Howard headed home. When he got there, Jonathan was already at the house waiting for him. He thought the Jamaican restaurant was a good idea, so they headed out. They went there in short order and sat back near the kitchen. They looked over the menu, and Howard decided to try a different dish tonight. Jonathan decided on a Jamaican version of shepherd's pie. He started to tell Howard about the trip he had just returned from.

Howard was listening with great interest, but then the door opened for another customer. Howard turned and recognized the man who his coworker had been with earlier. This time he was with another man. Howard watched the two men take a table near the front door. Jonathan noticed Howard paying attention to the new customers and asked if he knew them. Howard responded that he didn't but that he had seen one of them before. Jonathan indicated that the one Howard didn't recognize looked like a man who had been arrested on charges of spying for the Nazis a few weeks before but had been released because of lack of evidence. The word was that he had lost his job at the plant where Howard worked, however. Howard thought that this was consistent with what he had seen lately and thought he would talk to his manager in the morning.

That evening, Howard and Claudia were relaxing at home with Claudia's brother Pierre and his girlfriend Alexa. On his way to Claudia and Pierre's house, Howard stopped at the local flower shop. He thought it would be a nice idea to present both ladies with a bouquet of flowers.

He wasn't sure what their favorite flowers were, but he decided forget-me-nots would be a good choice. He walked the rest of the way, quietly looking forward to seeing his lady. As he turned to go up the walk to the house, he met a young small-framed white girl headed in the same direction. He had not met Pierre's girlfriend yet, so he wasn't sure if this was her headed to the house.

As the two stood side by side on the walk leading to the front door, the door opened, and Claudia stepped out. She was looking good. He handed both ladies their flowers, and they went in together. Pierre was in the living room and smiled broadly as they all came in.

"Flowers, very nice," he said. "I meant to get some, and now I am glad I didn't. I see you and Alexa have met."

Howard reached for Claudia to kiss her hello, and she held him warmly. The men sat down in the living room to enjoy a cigar, while the women retreated to the kitchen to work on dinner. Alexa was from Switzerland, so dinner would be a mixed meal of Swedish meatballs and plantains with some rum. The four of them enjoyed dinner together, and Pierre walked Alexa home. Howard stayed and helped Claudia clean up, and they talked about how Pierre and Alexa had met.

Claudia and Pierre had spent a Saturday going to the museum, and she was sitting out front waiting to meet a friend who hadn't shown up, and Pierre asked her to join them, and they hit it off and had been together ever since. Alexa did not have a lot of experience with men, or people for that matter, from other parts of the world, so when she met Pierre, she was fascinated with his manner and his accent. When Pierre threw on the charm, she couldn't resist. They had been each other's significant other for about six months now. People in Switzerland took great pride in their neutrality, but privately, Alexa's family had been very anti-Nazi, and if she had a chance to do something for the Allies, it was pretty certain that she would.

Chapter 13

The next day was Howard's first day in his new role at work. He looked at the staff at each workstation and asked about abilities and preferences. He thought some changes were appropriate and decided to slowly make changes to evaluate the new assignments as they happened. There had been reports from the air corps that a percentage of the bombs had failed to explode when dropped. The assembly procedures should not have caused or allowed this to happen, so a final quality appraisal review procedure might be called for. Howard decided this could be a good place for him to join the assembly procedure.

The next day, Howard reported to work and thought he would mainly observe the other workers to get an understanding of the workflow and look to find the best work teams as well as try to find where the problem was that was causing the detonation errors. There were five three-man teams in Howard's group. Each team had a separate responsibility in the production of the bombs. Team one's job was to prepare the explosive cavity for the TNT, making sure there was no interference to the bombs' detonation. Team two prepared and inserted the TNT into the bomb cavity. Team three built and prepared the detonator for insertion into the cavity alongside the TNT. Team four inserted the detonator, and finally, team five did a quality assurance check on the completed bomb.

Howard decided he would work with each of the teams one day for the first week and see if there were any problems with the process that could be resolved. Today he was working with team two. This was a group of people who seemed dedicated and careful. Handling the TNT, they needed to be precise and meticulous. This was not the step to try and speed up to increase the output. The day went well. The team worked well together, and they all seemed dedicated to getting the job done correctly and as quickly as they can.

The second day, he worked with team four. This team worked with the detonator. One of the team members was familiar to Howard. This was the man he had seen in the restaurant days before. Howard watched the flow carefully. The workers were careful to prime and place the detonators with just enough exposure outside of the TNT but inside of the bomb casing. It was a pressure-activated ignition, so the proper placement was important. Howard thought this was one of the most meticulous segments of the assembly process, so it was one with the most likely error opportunities.

The next day was his day to work with the quality assessment team. These folks were supposed to find any errors with the bombs before they left the assembly group. Howard decided to implement an additional step in the process to create a little more accountability. Each team would be increased by one member. The QA team would be split up, and one member would join each of the other groups. The QA member would inspect each bomb before it left that group rather than at the end of the process. This way, the errors could be discovered as they occurred rather than at the end of the entire process, hopefully enabling the management to see exactly where the weak link was. There was very little resistance to the new process. As a matter of fact, only two workers resisted at all and one was the man Howard and management had been watching.

Howard called for a meeting of team leaders to discuss the changes after they had been in place for the first week. It was noticed that the QA team member assigned to the detonator group went out of his way to handle each bomb before it left the plant, supposedly to double-check the detonator. Howard went behind him and found that the firing pins had been removed on approximately every fourth bomb, making them incapable of explosion. This was too regular of an oddity to be accidental, so he decided to reassign the QA man from this group if the error rate didn't improve immediately. Howard's manager came to see him at the end of the day to ask him for an update on how he thought things were going. Howard filled him in on how he thought the teams were working well together and how he thought there was a weak spot in one of the groups that he was going to watch for a few days and make a change if the situation didn't improve right away. The manager thought it was a good idea to give the situation a little time before making the changes but suggested Howard keep a close eye on all the team members. Howard agreed.

At the end of the day, Howard met with Claudia and filled her in on the day's events. She told him that her brother Pierre had told her that Alexa had mentioned that some of her coworkers had started to feel uneasy about one of their coworkers recently as well. She mentioned that it was the man they had seen with the suspected saboteur at Howard's plant. Howard decided that he would relay all this information to the military officer at his plant. He felt that a lot of this information was just too coincidental to be unimportant. He told Alexa he would arrange to have lunch the next day with the officer and they would fill him in about the suspected saboteurs.

Lunch was arranged the next day, and Howard, the military officer, and Alexa met at a bistro called Starlucks. Major Vanderbilt started the meeting by saying, "I am sure we have a saboteur in your group, Howard, and with your help, our investigators are pretty sure who it is. What we need to do next is decide how to address it. We need to act fast. We will be ready to arrest these guys as soon as they come into the plant in the morning. Finish up today as normal, but in the morning, call for a staff meeting first thing, and we will be in position to get them then."

Howard agreed, and the plan was set. His experience as a merchant marine and the strength he showed since his arrival at the munitions plant gave the military liaison officer and his superiors confidence in Howard as an inside man they needed to break the ring.

Chapter 14

The afternoon went by quickly, and the plant seemed to close as normal. Howard went to Claudia's house and sat with Claudia, Pierre, and Alexa. Not long after the group sat down for the evening, there was an explosion that seemed to come from the direction of the plant.

Howard said to Pierre, "What the hell was that?"

"It sounded like an explosion, and it seemed to come from the direction of the plant. Let's go see what it was."

The two men began walking toward the plant, and several others were moving in the plant's direction as well. The anticipated explosion had startled many other citizens as well. When they got to the plant, a crowd had gathered along the fence, but authorities would not allow anyone, except properly-credentialed people like Howard, inside the fence. The area where Howard had been working inside the plant was smoldering. There was nothing left of the building where his teams had worked. Howard identified himself to the fire marshals on site. They pointed out an area where it seemed the explosion had taken place and asked Howard if there was anything there that could have caused the explosion. Howard indicated that nothing to his recollection would have been there to cause an explosion.

He walked through the debris, kicking it as he walked through, looking for any clues that might show up. It seemed there was nothing to start the explosion, but still, Howard wondered, since there was nothing that could have accidentally caused the explosion, could there have been any reason anyone would intentionally cause the explosion?

He would check with the security guard at the gate and see if there was anything unusual that happened late in the day or shortly before the explosion.

The security guard was still at the entrance to the plant grounds, so Howard would check with him on his way out. He would check the sign-out sheet for his department as well. As he walked across the plant grounds, he saw the military officer who he had met with earlier and who he planned to meet with in the morning. "Hey, Howard. Is everybody OK?"

Howard told him that he was not aware of any injuries. As far as he knew, everyone had left for the day when the explosion happened.

"Well, I will look around a little more, but let's still meet tomorrow morning about the matter we discussed earlier."

Howard agreed that he would see the officer in the morning and turned to go toward the gate to leave. He asked the guard at the gate if he had noticed anything unusual as the day ended. The guard who was at the gate said that Old Pete had been on duty at the end of the day yesterday. They had not seen him when they came on duty this morning.

As Howard picked up the sign-out sheet, the guard noted that nothing has caught his attention. Howard looked at the sheet, and everyone had signed out from his department, but the order was unusual. As with any job, there were workers who usually left early and those who were usually the last to leave. Today the last name on the list was Stephen Johanson, usually one of the first two or three to leave. He was also one of the people suspected of sabotage who they were going to meet with in the morning. Howard noted the oddity and left for home and thought of all that he might discover in the morning's meeting.

The next morning, Howard arrived at the site of the plant earlier than usual. It was his plan to meet all his workers as they came onto the property and direct them to the conference room in the administration building. The crew came in slowly a couple at a time. Howard directed the crew members to the coffee wagon first and then told them to make their way to the conference room. The military liaison officer showed up next. He went straight to the conference room and began taking role.

When Howard joined him in the conference room, all the employees were present and accounted for, except Stephen Johanson and his friend Mikal Smith, the two who were to be the subject of the inquiry. Howard asked the group if anyone knew where they were. One employee spoke up and said that Stephan had stayed late yesterday, which surprised him, and that his partner had signed out but was waiting for him by the gate. With neither of them reporting to work this morning, there were talks of them being saboteurs. The military liaison officer spoke up and told the group not to jump to conclusions but that the two were suspects in a national security hunt.

One of the plant's maintenance engineers came into the conference room with a rather stressed look on his face. He asked Howard to come outside with him. Howard followed him out, and the man told Howard as soon as they were outside that Old Pete's body had been found behind building number 2 with a gunshot to his head. Howard returned to the meeting room with the thought that now, they were looking for not only saboteurs but also murderers. Pete had been a World War I veteran who wanted to help in any way he could in the war effort. Howard asked the group to notify him immediately if they saw either of the two men.

The munitions plant made plans to move operations to another facility. The Allies needed the production of this plant to continue if they were going to defeat the Nazis. The workers were told to report daily, and they would be back at munitions production as quickly as it could be arranged. Howard and some of the other managers stayed to help get things organized so that the rebuilding could get started as soon as possible. Later that day, when the men were tired and dirty, Howard left and went home to clean up. He looked forward to seeing Claudia. He went to her house and hoped to have a quiet evening with his lady. Pierre and Alexa were there as well, and they began the conversation about the plant explosion.

"What the heck happened at your plant Howard?"

"Well, we aren't sure, but we think it was intentionally destroyed. We had our eyes on a couple of guys that we thought were saboteurs. We aren't sure where they are now, but they didn't show up to work today."

Alexa sat up straight. "Do you mean the two guys you and I talked about the other day? You know they are both from Switzerland. Our watch company has a practice of welcoming any people that are here and from Switzerland and finding work in the watch plant for them. I will watch for them and see if they show up and let Pierre know if I see them or hear anything about new employees."

Howard had had enough conversation about the plant for one day and asked the group to change the subject.

***

That evening in another part of town, Bill Rogers, the military liaison officer, was talking with his superiors by phone. He had identified an abandoned building where the replacement plant could be set up. His superiors said they would decide to obtain the building and begin sending the equipment that would be needed. He was to keep his focus on trying to find the saboteurs.

***

The next morning, Howard woke to the smell of breakfast and the sound of birds singing to the dawn of a new day. Pierre and Alexa were already up as well. The quartet was ready to begin their day. Howard went to the destroyed plant site to try and help organize the inventory of what could be salvaged and moved to the next site once it was identified and prepared for the resumption of activity.

Alexa went to the watch factory with no particular expectations, but her day was not to be as void of activity as she anticipated. She went to the shipping department to talk with her friend who was the department head and asked about any new workers who might show up. He told her that there were two new applicants that he was to interview later that morning. They were both interested in signing up and joining the company to travel and move with deliveries to Germany or pickups in Switzerland. He told Alexa what time the interviews were scheduled to take place, and she made note so that she could be near the shipping department to catch a glimpse of the candidates. Just before lunch,

Alexa took her morning break and walked past the administrative offices where the personnel offices were located and then to the shipping department. She saw both candidates. They were indeed the same two men that she and Pierre had seen at the plant just days before.

That afternoon, she hurried to tell Pierre what she had found. Pierre went to tell Howard and plan their next move. Howard got in touch with Bill Rogers as the military liaison. Bill and his coworkers got in touch with the watch company and asked them to hire the two suspects and then got the schedule for the next shipment to Germany. The next shipment was due to go out at the end of that week. The week seemed to go by quickly as they anticipated arrest of the saboteurs.

On Friday morning, the shipment was readied, and the watch company employees prepared to leave. The truck was loaded with the shipment and the men, including the saboteurs. They headed to the dock where they would board the ferry that would take them to France. Bill Rogers and his men had arrived earlier. Bill and Howard were already on the ferry and had located themselves on the second level. Motorized passenger vehicles were next, and the watch company truck was third to board the ferry. Howard and Bill watched from the second level to see if the crew would get out of the truck or just sit tight for the short trip.

A couple of the men got out of the truck and walked to the ferry side rail. They lit up cigars and just looked out over the water. Howard and Bill kept an eye on the truck to see where the saboteurs went if anywhere. Bill had not told Howard all the plans for arresting the men, so he wasn't sure what would be happening next. Bill's men on the first level were watching the truck and its occupants.

The ferry approached the dock, and Bill's men followed the truck as it was in line to exit the ferry. When the truck reached the land, the first two vehicles were directed to exit to the left, and the cargo truck from the watch factory was directed to the right. An official truck blocked the path of the watch company truck. Officials surrounded the truck and told all the occupants to get out and lie facedown on the ground in front of the truck. The men did not hesitate and did as they were told. The officials identified the saboteurs and separated them from the other men. They were put in restraints and taken to the ferry for the ride back to Liverpool for the trial. The trial would take place in a week. The townspeople would be happy to try these accused saboteurs. Lives had been lost, as well as livelihoods, when the plant was destroyed. The trial was quick, and the anti-Nazi climate was apparent as a guilty verdict and the punishment phase came quickly.

Howard and Claudia felt good for the part they had played in stopping the Nazis in Liverpool. The war wasn't over, but maybe fewer Allies would die as a result of their activities.

CPSIA information can be obtained
at www.ICGtesting.com
Printed in the USA
BVHW031055090120
569086BV00001B/123/P